e

ELEGIES

Selected by
Ian Hamilton

BLOOMSBURY
* POETRY *
CLASSICS

This selection by Ian Hamilton first published 1997
Copyright © 1997 by Bloomsbury Publishing Plc
Bloomsbury Publishing Plc, 38 Soho Square,
London W1V 5DF

A CIP catalogue record for this book
is available from the British Library

ISBN 0 7475 3730 5

10 9 8 7 6 5 4 3 2 1

Typeset in Great Britain by
Hewer Text Composition Services, Edinburgh
Printed in Great Britain by St Edmundsbury Press, Suffolk
Jacket design by Jeff Fisher

CONTENTS

JOHN DONNE
A Funerall Elegie

Tis lost, to trust a Tombe with such a ghest,
  Or to confine her in a Marble chest.
Alas, what's Marble, Jeat, or Porphiry,
  Priz'd with the Chrysolite of eyther eye,
Or with those Pearles, and Rubies which shee was?
  Joyne the two Indies in one Tombe, 'tis glas;
And so is all to her materials,
  Though every inche were ten escurials.
Yet shee's demolish'd: Can we keepe her then
  In workes of hands, or of the wits of men?
Can these memorials, ragges of paper, give
  Life to that name, by which name they must live?
Sickly, alas, short-liv'd, aborted bee
  Those Carkas verses, whose soule is not shee.
And can shee, who no longer would be shee,
  Being such a Tabernacle, stoope to bee
In paper wrap't; Or, when she would not lie
  In such a house, dwell in an Elegie?
But 'tis no matter; we may well allow
  Verse to live so long as the world will now.
For her death wounded it. The world containes
  Princes for armes, and Counsailors for braines,
Lawyers for tongues. Divines for hearts, and more,
  The Rich for stomachs, and for backes the Pore;
The Officers for hands, Merchants for feet
  By which remote and distant Countries meet.

But those fine spirits, which doe tune and set
　　This Organ, are those peeces which beget
Wonder and love; And these were shee; and shee
　　Being spent, the world must needes decrepit bee.
For since death will proceed to triumph still,
　　He can finde nothing, after her, to kill,
Except the world it selfe, so great as shee.
　　Thus brave and confident may Nature bee,
Death cannot give her such another blow,
　　Because shee cannot such another show.
But must we say shee's dead? May't not be said
　　That as a sundred Clocke is peece-meale laid,
Not to be lost, but by the makers hand
　　Repolish'd, without error then to stand,
Or as the Affrique Niger streame enwombs
　　It selfe into the earth, and after comes,
(Having first made a naturall bridge, to passe
　　For many leagues,) farre greater then it was,
May't not be said, that her grave shall restore
　　Her, greater, purer, firmer, then before?
Heaven may say this, and joy in't; but can wee
　　Who live, and lacke her, here this vantage see?
What is't to us, alas, if there have beene
　　An Angell made a Throne, or Cherubin?
We lose by't: And as aged men are glad
　　Being tastelesse growne, to joy in joyes they had,
So now the sicke starv'd world must feed upone
　　This joy, that we had her, who now is gone.

Rejoyce then nature, and this world, that you
   Fearing the last fires hastning to subdue
Your force and vigor, ere it were neere gone,
   Wisely bestow'd, and layd it all on one.
One, whose cleare body was so pure, and thin,
   Because it neede disguise no thought within.
T'was but a through-light scarfe, her minde t'enroule,
   Or exhalation breath'd out from her soule.
One, whom all men who durst no more, admir'd;
   And whom, who ere had worth enough, desir'd;
As when a Temple's built, Saints emulate
   To which of them, it shall be consecrate.
But as when Heav'n lookes on us with new eyes,
   Those new starres ev'ry Artist exercise,
What place they should assigne to them they doubt,
   Argue, and agree not, till those starres go out:
So the world studied whose this peece should be,
   Till she can be no bodies else, nor shee:
But like a Lampe of Balsamum, desir'd
   Rather t'adorne, then last, shee soone expir'd;
Cloath'd in her Virgin white integrity;
   For mariage, though it doe not staine, doth dye.
To scape th'infirmities which waite upone
   Woman, shee went away, before sh'was one.
And the worlds busie noyse to overcome,
   Tooke so much death, as serv'd for *opium*.
For though she could not, nor could chuse to die,
   Shee'ath yeelded to too long an Extasie.

He which not knowing her sad History,
    Should come to reade the booke of destiny,
How faire, and chast, humble, and high shee'ad beene,
    Much promis'd, much perform'd, at not fifteene,
And measuring future things, by things before,
    Should turne the leafe to reade, and reade no more,
Would thinke that eyther destiny mistooke,
    Or that some leafes were torne out of the booke.
But 'tis not so: Fate did but usher her
    To yeares of Reasons use, and then infer
Her destiny to her selfe; which liberty
    She tooke but for thus much, thus much to die.
Her modesty not suffering her to bee
    Fellow-Commissioner with destinee,
Shee did no more but die; if after her
    Any shall live, which dare true good prefer,
Every such person is her delegate,
    T'accomplish that which should have beene her fate.
They shall make up that booke, and shall have thankes
    Of fate and her, for filling up their blanks.
For future vertuous deeds are Legacies,
    Which from the gift of her example rise.
And 'tis in heav'n part of spirituall mirth,
    To see how well, the good play her, on earth.

THOMAS CAREW
An Elegie upon the death of
Dr John Donne

Can we not force from widdowed Poetry,
Now thou art dead (Great DONNE) one Elegie
To crowne thy Hearse? Why yet dare we not trust
Though with unkneaded, dowe-bak't prose thy dust,
Such as the uncisor'd Churchman from the flower
Of fading Rhetorique, short liv'd as his houre,
Dry as the sand that measures it, should lay
Upon thy Ashes, on the funerall day?
Have we no voice, no tune? Did'st thou dispense
Through all our language, both the words and sense?
'Tis a sad truth; The Pulpit may her plaine
And sober Christian precepts still retaine,
Doctrines it may, and wholesome Uses frame,
Grave Homilies, and Lectures, But the flame
Of thy brave Soule, (that shot such heat and light,
As burnt our earth, and made our darknesse bright,
Committed holy Rapes upon our Will,
Did through the eye the melting heart distill;
And the deepe knowledge of darke truths so teach,
As sense might judge, what phansie could not reach;)
Must be desir'd for ever. So the fire,
That fills with spirit and heat the Delphique quire,
Which kindled first by thy Promethean breath,
Glow'd here a while, lies quench't now in thy death;

The Muses garden with Pedantique weedes
O'rspred, was purg'd by thee; The lazie seeds
Of servile imitation throwne away;
And fresh invention planted, Thou didst pay
The debts of our penurious bankrupt age;
Licentious thefts, that make poëtique rage
A Mimique fury, when our soules must bee
Possest, or with Anacreons Extasie,
Or Pindars, not their owne; The subtle cheat
Of slie Exchanges, and the jugling feat
Of two-edg'd words, or whatsoever wrong
By ours was done the Greeke, or Latine tongue,
Thou hast redeem'd, and open'd Us a Mine
Of rich and pregnant phansie, drawne a line
Of masculine expression, which had good
Old Orpheus seene, Or all the ancient Brood
Our superstitious fooles admire, and hold
Their lead more precious, than thy burnish't Gold,
Thou hadst been their Exchequer, and no more
They in each others dust, had rak'd for Ore.
Thou shalt yield no precedence, but of time,
And the blinde fate of language, whose tun'd chime
More charmes the outward sense; Yet thou maist
    claime
From so great disadvantage greater fame,
Since to the awe of thy imperious wit
Our stubborne language bends, made only fit
With her tough-thick-rib'd hoopes to gird about
Thy Giant phansie, which had prov'd too stout

For their soft melting Phrases. As in time
They had the start, so did they cull the prime
Buds of invention many a hundred yeare,
And left the rifled fields, besides the feare
To touch their Harvest, yet from those bare lands
Of what is purely thine, thy only hands
(And that thy smallest worke) have gleaned more
Than all those times, and tongues could reape before.

    But thou art gone, and thy strict lawes will be
Too hard for Libertines in Poetrie.
They will repeale the goodly exil'd traine
Of gods and goddesses, which in thy just raigne
Were banish'd nobler Poems, now, with these
The silenc'd tales o'th'Metamorphoses
Shall stuffe their lines, and swell the windy Page,
Till Verse refin'd by thee, in this last Age,
Turne ballad rime, Or those old Idolls bee
Ador'd againe, with new apostasie;

    Oh, pardon mee, that breake with untun'd verse
The reverend silence that attends thy herse,
Whose awfull solemne murmures were to thee
More than these faint lines, A loud Elegie,
That did proclaime in a dumbe eloquence
The death of all the Arts, whose influence
Growne feeble, in these panting numbers lies
Gasping short winded Accents, and so dies:
So doth the swiftly turning wheele not stand
In th'instant we withdraw the moving hand,

13

But some small time maintaine a faint weake course
By vertue of the first impulsive force:
And so whil'st I cast on thy funerall pile
Thy crowne of Bayes, Oh, let it crack a while,
And spit disdaine, till the devouring flashes
Suck all the moysture up, then turne to ashes.
    I will not draw the envy to engrosse
All thy perfections, or weepe all our losse;
Those are too numerous for an Elegie,
And this too great, to be express'd by mee.
Though every pen should share a distinct part,
Yet thou art Theme enough to tyre all Art;
Let others carve the rest, it shall suffice
I on thy Tombe this Epitaph incise.
> *Here lies a King, that rul'd as hee thought fit*
> *The universall Monarchy of wit;*
> *Here lie two Flamens, and both those, the best,*
> *Apollo's first, at last, the true God's Priest.*

BEN JONSON
To the Memory of William Shakespeare

To draw no envy (*Shakespeare*) on thy name,
  Am I thus ample to thy Booke, and Fame:
While I confesse thy writings to be such,
  As neither *Man*, nor *Muse*, can praise too much.
'Tis true, and all mens suffrage. But these wayes
  Were not the paths I meant unto thy praise:
For seeliest Ignorance on these may light,
  Which, when it sounds at best, but eccho's right;
Or blinde Affection, which doth ne'er advance
  The truth, but gropes, and urgeth all by chance:
Or crafty Malice, might pretend this praise,
  And thinke to ruine, where it seem'd to raise.
These are, as some infamous Baud, or whore,
  Should praise a Matron. What could hurt her more?
But thou art proofe against them, and indeed
  Above th'ill fortune of them, or the need.
I, therefore will begin. Soule of the Age!
  The applause! delight! the wonder of our Stage!
My *Shakespeare*, rise; I will not lodge thee by
  Chaucer, or *Spenser*, or bid *Beaumont* lye
A little further, to make thee a roome:
  Thou art a Moniment, without a tombe,
And art alive still, while thy Booke doth live,
  And we have wits to read, and praise to give.

That I not mixe thee so, my braine excuses;
    I meane with great, but disproportion'd *Muses*,
For, if I thought my judgement were of yeeres,
    I should commit thee surely with thy peeres,
And tell, how farre thou didst our *Lily* out-shine,
    Or sporting *Kid*, or *Marlowes* mighty line,
And though thou hadst small *Latine*, and lesse *Greeke*,
    From thence to honour thee I would not seeke
For names; but call forth thundring *Æschilus*,
    Euripides, and *Sophocles* to us,
Paccuvius, *Accius*, him of *Cordova* dead,
    To life againe, to heare thy Buskin tread,
And shake a Stage: Or, when thy Sockes were on,
    Leave thee alone, for the comparison
Of all, that insolent *Greece*, or haughtie *Rome*
    Sent forth, or since did from their ashes come.
Triumph, my *Britaine*, thou hast one to showe,
    To whom all Scenes of *Europe* homage owe.
He was not of an age, but for all time!
    And all the *Muses* still were in their prime,
When like *Apollo* he came forth to warme
    Our eares, or like a *Mercury* to charme!
Nature her selfe was proud of his designes,
    And joy'd to weare the dressing of his lines!
Which were so richly spun, and woven so fit,
    As, since, she will vouchsafe no other Wit.
The merry *Greeke*, tart *Aristophanes*,
    Neat *Terence*, witty *Plautus*, now not please;

JOHN MILTON
On the Morning of Christ's Nativity

I

This is the month, and this the happy morn
Wherein the Son of Heaven's eternal King,
Of wedded maid and virgin mother born,
Our great redemption from above did bring;
For so the holy sages once did sing,

That he our deadly forfeit should release,
And with his Father work us a perpetual peace.

II

That glorious form, that light unsufferable,
And that far-beaming blaze of majesty,
Wherewith he wont at Heaven's high council-table
To sit the midst of Trinal Unity,
He laid aside; and here with us to be,

Forsook the courts of everlasting day,
And chose with us a darksome house of mortal clay.

III

Say Heavenly Muse, shall not thy sacred vein
Afford a present to the Infant God?
Hast thou no verse, no hymn, or solemn strain,
To welcome him to this his new abode,
Now while the heaven, by the sun's team untrod,

Hath took no print of the approaching light,
And all the spangled host keep watch in squadrons
bright?

IV

See how from far upon the eastern road
The star-led wizards haste with odours sweet.
O run, prevent them with thy humble ode,
And lay it lowly at his blessed feet;
Have thou the honour first thy Lord to greet,
   And join thy voice unto the Angel quire
From out his secret altar toucht with hallowed fire.

The Hymn
I

It was the winter wild,
While the Heaven-born child
All meanly wrapt in the rude manger lies;
Nature in awe to him
Had doffed her gaudy trim,
With her great Master so to sympathize:
It was no season then for her
To wanton with the sun, her lusty paramour.

II

Only with speeches fair
She woos the gentle air
To hide her guilty front with innocent snow,
And on her naked shame,
Pollute with sinful blame,
The saintly veil of maiden white to throw,
Confounded that her Maker's eyes
Should look so near upon her foul deformities.

III

But he her fears to cease,
Sent down the meek-eyed Peace,
She crowned with olive green came softly sliding
Down through the turning sphere
His ready harbinger,
With turtle wing the amorous clouds dividing,
And waving wide her myrtle wand
She strikes a universal peace through sea and land.

IV

No war, or battle's sound
Was heard the World around,
The idle spear and shield were high up hung;
The hooked chariot stood
Unstained with hostile blood,
The trumpet spake not to the armed throng;
And kings sat still with awful eye,
As if they surely knew their sovereign lord was by.

V

But peaceful was the night
Wherein the Prince of light
His reign of peace upon the earth began.
The winds with wonder whist
Smoothly the waters kissed,
Whispering new joys to the mild Ocean,
Who now hath quite forgot to rave,
While birds of calm sit brooding on the charmed wave.

VI

The stars with deep amaze
Stand fixed in steadfast gaze,
Bending one way their precious influence,
And will not take their flight,
For all the morning light,
Or Lucifer that often warned them thence;
But in their glimmering orbs did glow,
Until their Lord himself bespake and bid them go.

VII

And though the shady gloom
Had given day her room,
The sun himself withheld his wonted speed,
And hid his head for shame,
As his inferior flame
The new enlightened world no more should need;
He saw a greater sun appear
Than his bright throne or burning axletree could bear.

VIII

The shepherds on the lawn,
Or ere the point of dawn,
Sat simply chatting in a rustic row;
Full little thought they then
That the mighty Pan
Was kindly come to live with them below;
Perhaps their loves, or else their sheep,
Was all that did their silly thoughts so busy keep.

IX

When such music sweet
Their hearts and ears did greet,
As never was by mortal finger strook,
Divinely-warbled voice
Answering the stringed noise,
As all their souls in blissful rapture took.
The air such pleasure loth to lose
With thousand echoes still prolongs each heavenly close.

X

Nature that heard such sound
Beneath the hollow round
Of Cynthia's seat the airy region thrilling,
Now was almost won
To think her part was done
And that her reign had here its last fulfilling;
She knew such harmony alone
Could hold all Heaven and Earth in happier union.

XI

At last surrounds their sight
A globe of circular light,
That with long beams the shamed-faced night arrayed;
The helmed cherubim
And sworded seraphim
Are seen in glittering ranks with wings displayed,
Harping in loud and solemn quire
With unexpressive notes to Heaven's new-born heir.

XII

Such music (as 'tis said)
Before was never made,
But when of old the sons of morning sung,
While the Creator great
His constellations set,
And the well-balanced world on hinges hung,
And cast the dark foundations deep,
And bid the weltering waves their oozy channel keep.

XIII

Ring out ye crystal spheres,
Once bless our human ears
(If ye have power to touch our senses so)
And let your silver chime
Move in melodious time;
And let the bass of Heaven's deep organ blow,
And with your ninefold harmony
Make up full consort to th'angelic symphony.

XIV

For if such holy song
Enwrap our fancy long,
Time will run back, and fetch the age of gold,
And speckled vanity
Will sicken soon and die,
And leprous sin will melt from earthly mould,
And Hell itself will pass away,
And leave her dolorous mansions to the peering day.

XV

Yea truth and justice then
Will down return to men,
Orbed in a rainbow; and like glories wearing
Mercy will sit between
Throned in celestial sheen,
With radiant feet the tissued clouds down steering,
And Heaven as at some festival,
Will open wide the gates of her high palace hall.

XVI

But wisest Fate says no,
This must not yet be so,
The babe lies yet in smiling infancy,
That on the bitter cross
Must redeem our loss;
So both himself and us to glorify.
Yet first to those ychained in sleep
The wakeful trump of doom must thunder through the deep,

XVII

With such a horrid clang
As on Mount Sinai rang
While the red fire and smouldering clouds out brake.
The aged earth aghast
With terror of that blast
Shall from the surface to the centre shake,
When at the world's last session
The dreadful Judge in middle air shall spread his throne.

XVIII

And then at last our bliss
Full and perfect is,
But now begins; for from this happy day
Th'old dragon underground
In straiter limits bound,
Not half so far casts his usurped sway,
And wrath to see his kingdom fail
Swindges the scaly horror of his folded tail.

XIX

The oracles are dumb,
No voice or hideous hum
Runs through the arched roof in words deceiving.
Apollo from his shrine
Can no more divine,
With hollow shriek the steep of Delphos leaving.
No nightly trance, or breathed spell,
Inspires the pale-eyed priest from the prophetic cell.

XX

The lonely mountains o'er,
And the resounding shore,
A voice of weeping heard and loud lament;
From haunted spring, and dale
Edged with poplar pale,
The parting genius is with sighing sent;
With flower-inwoven tresses torn
The nymphs in twilight shade of tangled thickets mourn.

XXI

In consecrated earth,
And on the holy hearth,
The Lars and Lemures moan with midnight plaint,
In urns and altars round,
A drear and dying sound
Affrights the flamens at their service quaint;
And the chill marble seems to sweat,
While each peculiar power forgoes his wonted seat.

XXII

Peor and Baalim
Forsake their temples dim,
With that twice-battered god of Palestine,
And mooned Ashtaroth,
Heaven's queen and mother both,
Now sits not girt with tapers' holy shine;
The Libyc Hammon shrinks his horn,
In vain the Tyrian maids their wounded Thammuz mourn.

XXIII

And sullen Moloch fled,
Hath left in shadows dread
His burning idol all of blackest hue;
In vain with cymbals' ring
They call the grisly king,
In dismal dance about the furnace blue;
The brutish gods of Nile as fast,
Isis and Orus and the dog Anubis haste.

XXIV

Nor is Osiris seen
In Memphian grove or green,
Trampling the unshowered grass with lowings loud;
Nor can he be at rest
Within his sacred chest,
Nought but profoundest Hell can be his shroud;
In vain with timbrelled anthems dark
The sable-stoled sorcerers bear his worshipped ark.

XXV

He feels from Juda's land
The dreaded infant's hand,
The rays of Bethlehem blind his dusky eyn;
Nor all the gods beside
Longer dare abide,
Not Typhon huge ending in snaky twine.
Our babe to show his godhead true
Can in his swaddling bands control the damned crew.

XXVI

So when the sun in bed,
Curtained with cloudy red,
Pillows his chin upon an orient wave,
The flocking shadows pale
Troop to th'infernal jail,
Each fettered ghost slips to his several grave,
And the yellow-skirted fays
Fly after the night-steeds, leaving their moon-loved maze.

XXVII

But see the Virgin blest
Hath laid her babe to rest.
Time is our tedious song should here have ending;
Heaven's youngest teemed star
Hath fixed her polished car,
Her sleeping Lord with handmaid lamp attending;
And all about the courtly stable
Bright-harnessed angels sit in order serviceable.

ANDREW MARVELL
An Horation Ode upon Cromwell's Return from Ireland

The forward youth that would appear
Must now forsake his muses dear,
   Nor in the shadows sing
   His numbers languishing.
'Tis time to leave the books in dust,
And oil the unusèd armour's rust:
   Removing from the wall
   The corslet of the hall.
So restless Cromwell could not cease
In the inglorious arts of peace,
   But through adventurous war
   Urgèd his active star.
And, like the three-forked lightning, first
Breaking the clouds where it was nursed,
   Did thorough his own side
   His fiery way divide.
(For 'tis all one to courage high
The emulous or enemy:
   And with such to inclose
   Is more than to oppose.)

Then burning through the air he went,
And palaces and temples rent:
   And Caesar's head at last
   Did through his laurels blast.
'Tis madness to resist or blame
The force of angry heaven's flame:
   And, if we would speak true,
   Much to the man is due,
Who, from his private gardens, where
He lived reservèd and austere,
   As if his highest plot
   To plant the bergamot,
Could by industrious valour climb
To ruin the great work of time,
   And cast the kingdoms old
   Into another mould.
Though justice against fate complain,
And plead the ancient rights in vain:
   But those do hold or break
   As men are strong or weak.
Nature, that hateth emptiness,
Allows of penetration less:
   And therefore must make room
   Where greater spirits come.

What field of all the Civil Wars,
Where his were not the deepest scars?
   And Hampton shows what part
   He had of wiser art,
Where, twining subtle fears with hope,
He wove a net of such a scope,
   That Charles himself might chase
   To Carisbrooke's narrow case:
That thence the royal actor born
The tragic scaffold might adorn:
   While round the armèd bands
   Did clap their bloody hands.
He nothing common did or mean
Upon that memorable scene:
   But with his keener eye
   The axe's edge did try:
Nor called the gods with vulgar spite
To vindicate his helpless right,
   But bowed his comely head,
   Down, as upon a bed.
This was that memorable hour
Which first assured the forcèd power.
   So when they did design
   The Capitol's first line,

A bleeding head where they begun,
Did fright the architects to run;
   And yet in that the State
   Foresaw its happy fate.
And now the Irish are ashamed
To see themselves in one year tamed:
   So much one man can do,
   That does both act and know.
They can affirm his praises best,
And have, though overcome, confessed
   How good he is, how just,
   And fit for highest trust:
Nor yet grown stiffer with command,
But still in the Republic's hand:
   How fit he is to sway
   That can so well obey.
He to the Commons' feet presents
A kingdom, for his first year's rents:
   And, what he may, forbears
   His fame, to make it theirs:
And has his sword and spoils ungirt,
To lay them at the public's skirt.
   So when the falcon high
   Falls heavy from the sky,

She, having killed, no more does search
But on the next green bough to perch,
  Where, when he first does lure,
  The falc'ner has her sure.
What may not then our isle presume
While Victory his crest does plume?
  What may not others fear
  If thus he crowns each year?
A Caesar, he, ere long to Gaul,
To Italy an Hannibal,
  And to all states not free
  Shall climactéric be.
The Pict no shelter now shall find
Within his parti-coloured mind,
  But from this valour sad
  Shrink underneath the plaid:
Happy, if in the tufted brake
The English hunter him mistake,
  Nor lay his hounds in near
  The Caledonian deer.
But thou, the Wars' and Fortune's son,
March indefatigably on,
  And for the last effect
  Still keep thy sword erect:
Besides the force it has to fright
The spirits of the shady night,
  The same arts that did gain
  A power, must it maintain.

Fame is no plant that grows on mortal soil,
Nor in the glistering foil
Set off to th'world, nor in broad rumour lies,
But lives and spreads aloft by those pure eyes,
And perfect witness of all-judging Jove;
As he pronounces lastly on each deed,
Of so much fame in Heaven expect thy meed.

O fountain Arethuse, and thou honoured flood,
Smooth-sliding Mincius, crowned with vocal reeds,
That strain I heard was of a higher mood.
But now my oat proceeds,
And listens to the herald of the sea
That came in Neptune's plea;
He asked the waves, and asked the felon winds,
What hard mishap hath doomed this gentle swain?
And questioned every gust of rugged wings
That blows from off each beaked promontory;
They knew not of his story;
And sage Hippotades their answer brings,
That not a blast was from his dungeon strayed,
The air was calm, and on the level brine,
Sleek Panope with all her sisters played.
It was that fatal and perfidious bark
Built in th'eclipse, and rigged with curses dark,
That sunk so low that sacred head of thine.

Next Camus, reverend sire, went footing slow,
His mantle hairy, and his bonnet sedge,
Inwrought with figures dim, and on the edge

Like to that sanguine flower inscribed with woe.
Ah! who hath reft (quoth he) my dearest pledge?
Last came and last did go,
The pilot of the Galilean lake,
Two massy keys he bore of metals twain,
(The golden opes, the iron shuts amain)
He shook his mitred locks, and stern bespake,
How well could I have spared for thee, young swain,
Enow of such as for their bellies' sake,
Creep and intrude, and climb into the fold?
Of other care they little reckoning make,
Than how to scramble at the shearers' feast,
And shove away the worthy bidden guest.
Blind mouths! That scarce themselves know how to
    hold
A sheep-hook, or have learned ought else the least
That to the faithful herdsman's art belongs!
What recks it them? What need they? They are sped;
And when they list, their lean and flashy songs
Grate on their scrannel pipes of wretched straw;
The hungry sheep look up, and are not fed,
But swoln with wind, and the rank mist they draw,
Rot inwardly, and foul contagion spread:
Besides what the grim wolf with privy paw
Daily devours apace, and nothing said.
But that two-handed engine at the door,
Stands ready to smite once, and smite no more.
    Return Alpheus, the dread voice is past,

That shrunk thy streams; return Sicilian muse,
And call the vales, and bid them hither cast
Their bells, and flowerets of a thousand hues.
Ye valleys low where the mild whispers use,
Of shades and wanton winds, and gushing brooks,
On whose fresh lap the swart star sparely looks,
Throw hither all your quaint enamelled eyes,
That on the green turf suck the honeyed showers,
And purple all the ground with vernal flowers.
Bring the rathe primrose that forsaken dies.
The tufted crow-toe, and pale jessamine,
The white pink, and the pansy freaked with jet,
The glowing violet.
The musk-rose, and the well attired woodbine.
With cowslips wan that hang the pensive head,
And every flower that sad embroidery wears:
Bid amaranthus all his beauty shed,
And daffadillies fill their cups with tears,
To strew the laureate hearse where Lycid lies.
For so to interpose a little ease,
Let our frail thoughts dally with false surmise.
Ay me! Whilst thee the shores, and sounding seas
Wash far away, where e'er thy bones are hurled,
Whether beyond the stormy Hebrides,
Where thou perhaps under the whelming tide
Visit'st the bottom of the monstrous world;
Or whether thou to our moist vows denied,
Sleepst by the fable of Bellerus old,

Where the great vision of the guarded mount
Looks toward Namancos and Bayona's hold;
Look homeward angel now, and melt with ruth.
And, O ye dolphins, waft the hapless youth.

Weep no more, woeful shepherds, weep no more,
For Lycidas your sorrow is not dead,
Sunk though he be beneath the watery floor,
So sinks the day-star in the ocean bed,
And yet anon repairs his drooping head,
And tricks his beams, and with new spangled ore,
Flames in the forehead of the morning sky:
So Lycidas sunk low, but mounted high,
Through the dear might of him that walked the waves,
Where other groves, and other streams along,
With nectar pure his oozy locks he laves,
And hears the unexpressive nuptial song,
In the blest kingdoms meek of joy and love.
There entertain him all the saints above,
In solemn troops and sweet societies
That sing, and singing in their glory move,
And wipe the tears for ever from his eyes.
Now Lycidas the shepherds weep no more;
Henceforth thou art the genius of the shore,
In thy large recompense, and shalt be good
To all that wander in that perilous flood.

Thus sang the uncouth swain to th'oaks and rills,
While the still morn went out with sandals gray;
He touched the tender stops of various quills,
With eager thought warbling his Doric lay:

And now the sun had stretched out all the hills,
And now was dropt into the western bay;
At last he rose, and twitched his mantle blue:
To-morrow to fresh woods, and pastures new.

THOMAS GRAY
Elegy Written in a Country Churchyard

The curfew tolls the knell of parting day,
  The lowing herd winds slowly o'er the lea,
The plowman homeward plods his weary way,
  And leaves the world to darkness and to me.

Now fades the glimmering landscape on the sight,
  And all the air a solemn stillness holds,
Save where the beetle wheels his droning flight,
  And drowsy tinklings lull the distant folds;

Save that from yonder ivy-mantled tower
  The moping owl does to the moon complain
Of such as, wand'ring near her secret bower,
  Molest her ancient solitary reign.

Beneath those rugged elms, that yew-tree's shade,
  Where heaves the turf in many a mould'ring heap,
Each in his narrow cell for ever laid,
  The rude forefathers of the hamlet sleep.

The breezy call of incense-breathing morn,
  The swallow twitt'ring from the straw-built shed,
The cock's shrill clarion, or the echoing horn,
  No more shall rouse them from their lowly bed.

For them no more the blazing hearth shall burn,
  Or busy housewife ply her evening care:
No children run to lisp their sire's return,
  Or climb his knees the envied kiss to share.

Oft did the harvest to their sickle yield,
  Their furrow oft the stubborn glebe has broke:
How jocund did they drive their team afield!
  How bowed the woods beneath their sturdy stroke!

Let not Ambition mock their useful toil,
  Their homely joys, and destiny obscure;
Nor Grandeur hear with a disdainful smile
  The short and simple annals of the poor.

The boast of heraldry, the pomp of power,
  And all that beauty, all that wealth e'er gave,
Awaits alike th' inevitable hour:
  The paths of glory lead but to the grave.

Nor you, ye proud, impute to These the fault,
  If Memory o'er their tomb no trophies raise,
Where through the long-drawn aisle and fretted vault
  The pealing anthem swells the note of praise.

Can storied urn or animated bust
  Back to its mansion call the fleeting breath?
Can Honour's voice provoke the silent dust,
  Or Flatt'ry soothe the dull cold ear of death?

Perhaps in this neglected spot is laid
   Some heart once pregnant with celestial fire;
Hands, that the rod of empire might have swayed,
   Or waked to ecstasy the living lyre.

But Knowledge to their eyes her ample page
   Rich with the spoils of time did ne'er unroll;
Chill Penury repressed their noble rage,
   And froze the genial current of the soul.

Full many a gem of purest ray serene
   The dark unfathomed caves of ocean bear;
Full many a flower is born to blush unseen,
   And waste its sweetness on the desert air.

Some village Hampden that with dauntless breast
   The little tyrant of his fields withstood,
Some mute inglorious Milton here may rest,
   Some Cromwell guiltless of his country's blood.

Th' applause of list'ning senates to command,
   The threats of pain and ruin to despise,
To scatter plenty o'er a smiling land,
   And read their history in a nation's eyes,

Their lot forbade: nor circumscribed alone
   Their growing virtues, but their crimes confined;
Forbade to wade through slaughter to a throne.
   And shut the gates of mercy on mankind,

The struggling pangs of conscious truth to hide,
    To quench the blushes of ingenuous shame,
Or heap the shrine of Luxury and Pride
    With incense kindled at the Muse's flame.

Far from the madding crowd's ignoble strife
    Their sober wishes never learned to stray;
Along the cool sequestered vale of life.
    They kept the noiseless tenor of their way.

Yet ev'n these bones from insult to protect
    Some frail memorial still erected nigh,
With uncouth rhymes and shapeless sculpture decked,
    Implores the passing tribute of a sigh.

Their name, their years, spelt by th' unlettered Muse,
    The place of fame and elegy supply:
And many a holy text around she strews,
    That teach the rustic moralist to die.

For who, to dumb Forgetfulness a prey,
    This pleasing anxious being e'er resigned,
Left the warm precincts of the cheerful day,
    Nor cast one longing ling'ring look behind?

On some fond breast the parting soul relies,
    Some pious drops the closing eye requires;
E'en from the tomb the voice of Nature cries,
    E'en in our Ashes live their wonted fires.

For thee, who, mindful of th' unhonoured dead,
    Dost in these lines their artless tale relate;
If chance, by lonely contemplation led,
    Some kindred spirit shall inquire thy fate,

Haply some hoary-headed Swain may say,
    'Oft have we seen him at the peep of dawn
Brushing with hasty steps the dews away
    To meet the sun upon the upland lawn.

'There at the foot of yonder nodding beech
    That wreathes its old fantastic roots so high,
His listless length at noontide would he stretch,
    And pore upon the brook that babbles by.

'Hard by yon wood, now smiling as in scorn,
    Mutt'ring his wayward fancies he would rove,
Now drooping, woeful wan, like one forlorn,
    Or crazed with care, or crossed in hopeless love.

'One morn I missed him on the customed hill,
    Along the heath and near his fav'rite tree;
Another came; nor yet beside the rill,
    Nor up the lawn, nor at the wood was he;

'The next with dirges due in sad array
    Slow through the church-way path we saw him borne.
Approach and read (for thou canst read) the lay
    Graved on the stone beneath yon aged thorn:'

The Epitaph

Here rests his head upon the lap of Earth
  A Youth to Fortune and to Fame unknown.
Fair Science frowned not on his humble birth,
  And Melancholy marked him for her own.

Large was his bounty, and his soul sincere,
  Heaven did a recompense as largely send:
He gave to Mis'ry all he had, a tear,
  He gained from Heaven ('twas all he wished) a friend.

No further seek his merits to disclose,
  Or draw his frailties from their dread abode,
(There they alike in trembling hope repose,)
The bosom, of his Father and his God.

ALEXANDER POPE
Elegy to the Memory of an Unfortunate Lady

What beckoning ghost along the moonlight shade
Invites my steps, and points to yonder glade?
'Tis she! – but why that bleeding bosom gored,
Why dimly gleams the visionary sword?
Oh, ever beauteous, ever friendly! tell,
Is it, in heaven, a crime to love too well?
To bear too tender or too firm a heart,
To act a lover's or a Roman's part?
Is there no bright reversion in the sky
For those who greatly think, or bravely die?

Why bade ye else, ye powers! her soul aspire
Above the vulgar flight of low desire?
Ambition first sprung from your blest abodes,
The glorious fault of angels and of gods:
Thence to their images on earth it flows,
And in the breast of kings and heroes glows.
Most souls, 'tis true, but peep out once an age,
Dull, sullen prisoners in the body's cage:
Dim lights of life, that burn a length of years,
Useless, unseen, as lamps in sepulchres;
Like Eastern kings a lazy state they keep,
And, close confined to their own palace, sleep.

From these perhaps (ere Nature bade her die)
Fate snatched her early to the pitying sky.
As into air the purer spirits flow,
And separate from their kindred dregs below;

44

So flew soul to its congenial place,
Nor left one virtue to redeem her race,
    But thou, false guardian of a charge too good,
Thou, mean deserter of thy brother's blood!
See on these ruby lips the trembling breath,
These cheeks now fading at the blast of death;
Cold is that breast which warm'd the world before,
And those love-darting eyes must roll no more.
Thus, if eternal justice rules the ball,
Thus, shall your wives, and thus your children fall:
On all the line a sudden vengeance waits,
And frequent hearses shall besiege your gates;
There passengers shall stand, and pointing say,
(While the long funerals blacken all the way,)
'Lo! these were they, whose souls the Furies steel'd,
And cursed with hearts unknowing how to yield.'
    Thus unlamented pass the proud away,
The gaze of fools, and pageant of a day!
So perish all, whose breast ne'er learn'd to glow
For others' good, or melt at others' woe.
    What can atone (oh ever-injured shade!)
Thy fate unpitied, and thy rites unpaid?
No friend's complaint, no kind domestic tear
Pleased thy pale ghost, or graced thy mournful bier.
By foreign hands thy dying eyes were closed,
By foreign hands thy decent limbs composed,
By foreign hands thy humble grave adorn'd,
By strangers honour'd, and by strangers mourn'd!
What, though no friends in sable weeds appear,

Grieve for an hour, perhaps then mourn a year,
And bear about the mockery of woe
To midnight dances, and the public show?
What, though no weeping loves thy ashes grace,
Nor polish'd marble emulate thy face?
What, though no sacred earth allow thee room,
Nor hallow'd dirge be mutter'd o'er thy tomb?
Yet shall thy grave with rising flowers be dress'd
And the green turf lie lightly on thy breast:
There shall the morn her earliest tears bestow,
There the first roses of the year shall blow;
While angels with their silver wings o'ershade
The ground now sacred by thy reliques made.

So peaceful rests, without a stone, a name,
What once had beauty, titles, wealth, and fame.
How loved, how honour'd once, avails thee not,
To whom related, or by whom begot;
A heap of dust alone remains of thee,
'Tis all thou art, and all the proud shall be!

Poets themselves must fall, like those they sung,
Deaf the praised ear, and mute the tuneful tongue.
Even he, whose soul now melts in mournful lays,
Shall shortly want the generous tear he pays;
Then from his closing eyes thy form shall part,
And the last pang shall tear thee from his heart,
Life's idle business at one gasp be o'er,
The Muse forgot, and thou beloved no more!

LORD BYRON
Elegy on Thyrza

And thou art dead, as young and fair
  As aught of mortal birth;
And forms so soft and charms so rare
  Too soon return'd to Earth!
Though Earth received them in her bed,
And o'er the spot the crowd may tread
  In carelessness or mirth,
There is an eye which could not brook
A moment on that grave to look.

I will not ask where thou liest low
  Nor gaze upon the spot;
There flowers or weeds at will may grow
  So I behold them not:
It is enough for me to prove
That what I loved and long must love
  Like common earth can rot;
To me there needs no stone to tell
'Tis Nothing that I loved so well.

Yet did I love thee to the last,
    As fervently as thou
Who didst not change through all the past
    And canst not alter now.
The love where Death has set his seal
Nor age can chill, nor rival steal,
    Nor falsehood disavow:
And, what were worse, thou canst not see
Or wrong, or change, or fault in me.

The better days of life were ours;
    The worst can be but mine:
The sun that cheers, the storm that lours,
    Shall never more be thine.
The silence of that dreamless sleep
I envy now too much to weep;
    Nor need I to repine
That all those charms have pass'd away
I might have watch'd through long decay.

The flower in ripen'd bloom unmatch'd
    Must fall the earliest prey;
Though by no hand untimely snatch'd,
    The leaves must drop away.
And yet it were a greater grief
To watch it withering, leaf by leaf,
    Than see it pluck'd today;
Since earthly eye but ill can bear
To trace the change to foul from fair.

I know not if I could have borne
    To see thy beauties fade;
The night that follow'd such a morn
    Had worn a deeper shade:
Thy day without a cloud hath past,
And thou wert lovely to the last,
    Extinguish'd, not decay'd;
As stars that shoot along the sky
Shine brightest as they fall from high.

As once I wept, if I could weep,
    My tears might well be shed
To think I was not near, to keep
    One vigil o'er thy bed:
To gaze, how fondly! on thy face,
To fold thee in a faint embrace,
    Uphold thy drooping head;
And show that love, however vain,
Nor thou nor I can feel again.

Yet how much less it were to gain,
    Though thou hast left me free,
The loveliest things that still remain
    Than thus remember thee!
The all of thine that cannot die
Through dark and dread Eternity
    Returns again to me,
And more thy buried love endears
Than aught except its living years.

LORD BYRON
Elegy

O snatch'd away in beauty's bloom!
On thee shall press no ponderous tomb;
But on thy turf shall roses rear
Their leaves, the earliest of the year,
And the wild cypress wave in tender gloom:

And oft by yon blue gushing stream
Shall Sorrow lean her drooping head,
And feed deep thought with many a dream,
And lingering pause and lightly tread;
Fond wretch! as if her step disturb'd the dead!

Away! we know that tears are vain,
That Death nor heeds nor hears distress:
Will this unteach us to complain?
Or make one mourner weep the less?
And thou, who tell'st me to forget,
Thy looks are wan, thine eyes are wet.

WILLIAM WORDSWORTH
Elegiac Stanzas

Suggested by a Picture of Peele Castle, in a Storm, Painted by Sir
George Beaumont

I was thy neighbour once, thou rugged Pile!
Four summer weeks I dwelt in sight of thee:
I saw thee every day; and all the while
Thy Form was sleeping on a glassy sea.

So pure the sky, so quiet was the air!
So like, so very like, was day to day!
Whene'er I looked, thy Image still was there;
It trembled, but it never passed away.

How perfect was the calm! it seemed no sleep;
No mood, which season takes away, or brings:
I could have fancied that the mighty Deep
Was even the gentlest of all gentle Things.

Ah! then, if mine had been the Painter's hand,
To express what then I saw; and add the gleam,
The light that never was, on sea or land,
The consecration, and the Poet's dream;

I would have planted thee, thou hoary Pile!
Amid a world how different from this!
Beside a sea that could not cease to smile;
On tranquil land, beneath a sky of bliss:

Thou shouldst have seemed a treasure-house, a
    mine
Of peaceful years; a chronicle of heaven:-
Of all the sunbeams that did ever shine
The very sweetest had to thee been given.

A Picture had it been of lasting ease,
Elysian quiet, without toil or strife;
No motion but the moving tide, a breeze,
Or merely silent Nature's breathing life.

Such, in the fond delusion of my heart,
Such Picture would I at that time have made:
And seen the soul of truth in every part;
A faith, a trust, that could not be betrayed.

So once it would have been, - 'tis so no more;
I have submitted to a new controul:
A power is gone, which nothing can restore;
A deep distress hath humanized my Soul.

Not for a moment could I now behold
A smiling sea and be what I have been:
The feeling of my loss will ne'er be old;
This, which I know, I speak with mind serene.

Then, Beaumont, Friend! who would have been the
      Friend,
If he had lived, of Him whom I deplore,
This Work of thine I blame not, but commend;
This sea in anger, and the dismal shore.

Oh 'tis a passionate Work! – yet wise and well;
Well chosen is the spirit that is here;
That Hulk which labours in the deadly swell,
This rueful sky, this pageantry of fear!

And this huge Castle, standing here sublime,
I love to see the look with which it braves,
Cased in the unfeeling armour of old time,
The light'ning, the fierce wind, and trampling waves.

Farewell, farewell the Heart that lives alone,
Housed in a dream, at distance from the Kind!
Such happiness, wherever it be known,
Is to be pitied; for 'tis surely blind.

But welcome fortitude, and patient chear,
And frequent sights of what is to be borne!
Such sights, or worse, as are before me here. –
Not without hope we suffer and we mourn.

PERCY BYSSHE SHELLEY
From *Adonais*

I

I weep for Adonais – he is dead!
O, weep for Adonais! though our tears
Thaw not the frost which binds so dear a head!
And thou, sad Hour, selected from all years
To mourn our loss, rouse thy obscure compeers,
And teach them thine own sorrow, say: 'With me
Died Adonais; till the Future dares
Forget the Past, his fate and fame shall be
An echo and a light unto eternity!'

II

Where wert thou, mighty Mother, when he lay,
When thy Son lay, pierced by the shaft which flies
In darkness? where was lorn Urania
When Adonais died? With veilèd eyes,
'Mid listening Echoes, in her Paradise
She sate, while one, with soft enamoured breath,
Rekindled all the fading melodies,
With which, like flowers that mock the corse
    beneath,
He had adorned and hid the coming bulk of Death.

III

Oh, weep for Adonais – he is dead!
Wake, melancholy Mother, wake and weep!
Yet wherefore? Quench within their burning bed
Thy fiery tears, and let thy loud heart keep
Like his, a mute and uncomplaining sleep;
For he is gone, where all things wise and fair
Descend; – oh, dream not that the amorous Deep
Will yet restore him to the vital air;
Death feeds on his mute voice, and laughs at our
    despair.

IV

Most musical of mourners, weep again!
Lament anew, Urania! – He died,
Who was the Sire of an immortal strain,
Blind, old, and lonely, when his country's pride,
The priest, the slave, and the liberticide,
Trampled and mocked with many a loathèd rite
Of lust and blood; he went, unterrified,
Into the gulf of death; but his clear Sprite
Yet reigns o'er earth; the third among the sons of
    light.

V

Most musical of mourners, weep anew!
Not all to that bright station dared to climb;
And happier they their happiness who knew,
Whose tapers yet burn through that night of time
In which suns perished; others more sublime,
Struck by the envious wrath of man or god,
Have sunk, extinct in their refulgent prime;
And some yet live, treading the thorny road,
Which leads, through toil and hate, to Fame's serene
abode.

VI

But now, thy youngest, dearest one, has perished –
The nursling of thy widowhood, who grew,
Like a pale flower by some sad maiden cherished,
And fed with true-love tears, instead of dew;
Most musical of mourners, weep anew!
Thy extreme hope, the loveliest and the last,
The bloom, whose petals nipped before they blew
Died on the promise of the fruit, is waste;
The broken lily lies – the storm is overpast.

VII

To that high Capital, where kingly Death
Keeps his pale court in beauty and decay,
He came; and bought, with price of purest breath,
A grave among the eternal. – Come away!
Haste, while the vault of blue Italian day
Is yet his fitting charnel-roof! while still
He lies, as if in dewy sleep he lay;
Awake him not! surely he takes his fill
Of deep and liquid rest, forgetful of all ill.

VIII

He will awake no more, oh, never more! –
Within the twilight chamber spreads apace
The shadow of white Death, and at the door
Invisible Corruption waits to trace
His extreme way to her dim dwelling-place;
The eternal Hunger sits, but pity and awe
Soothe her pale rage, nor dares she to deface
So fair a prey, till darkness, and the law
Of change, shall o'er his sleep the mortal curtain draw.

IX

Oh, weep for Adonais! – The quick Dreams,
The passion-wingèd Ministers of thought,
Who were his flocks, whom near the living streams
Of his young spirit he fed, and whom he taught
The love which was its music, wander not, –
Wander no more, from kindling brain to brain,
But droop there, whence they sprung; and mourn
    their lot
Round the cold heart, where, after their sweet pain,
They ne'er will gather strength, or find a home again.

X

And one with trembling hands clasps his cold head,
And fans him with her moonlight wings, and cries;
'Our love, our hope, our sorrow, is not dead;
See, on the silken fringe of his faint eyes,
Like dew upon a sleeping flower, there lies
A tear some Dream has loosened from his brain.'
Lost Angel of a ruined Paradise!
She knew not 'twas her own; as with no stain
She faded, like a cloud which had outwept its rain.

XI

One from a lucid urn of starry dew
Washed his light limbs as if embalming them;
Another clipped her profuse locks, and threw
The wreath upon him, like an anadem,
Which frozen tears instead of pearls begem;
Another in her wilful grief would break
Her bow and wingèd reeds, as if to stem
A greater loss with one which was more weak;
And dull the barbèd fire against his frozen cheek.

XII

Another Splendour on his mouth alit,
That mouth, whence it was wont to draw the
    breath
Which gave it strength to pierce the guarded wit,
And pass into the panting heart beneath
With lightning and with music: the damp death
Quenched its caress upon his icy lips;
And, as a dying meteor stains a wreath
Of moonlight vapour, which the cold night clips,
It flushed through his pale limbs, and passed to its
    eclipse.

XIII

And others came . . . Desires and Adorations,
Wingèd Persuasions and veiled Destinies,
Splendours, and Glooms, and glimmering
    Incarnations
Of hopes and fears, and twilight Phantasies;
And Sorrow, with her family of Sighs,
And Pleasure, blind with tears, led by the gleam
Of her own dying smile instead of eyes,
Came in slow pomp; – the moving pomp might
    seem
Like pageantry of mist on an autumnal stream.

XIV

All he had loved, and moulded into thought,
From shape, and hue, and odour, and sweet sound,
Lamented Adonais. Morning sought
Her eastern watch-tower, and her hair unbound,
Wet with the tears which should adorn the ground,
Dimmed the aëreal eyes that kindle day;
Afar the melancholy thunder moaned,
Pale Ocean in unquiet slumber lay,
And the wild Winds flew round, sobbing in their
    dismay.

Lost Echo sits amid the voiceless mountains,
And feeds her grief with his remembered lay,
And will no more reply to winds or fountains,
Or amorous birds perched on the young green
    spray,
Or herdsman's horn, or bell at closing day;
Since she can mimic not his lips, more dear
Than those for whose disdain she pined away
Into a shadow of all sounds: – a drear
Murmur, between their songs, is all the woodmen
  hear.

XVI

Grief made the young Spring wild, and she threw
    down
Her kindling buds, as if she Autumn were,
Or they dead leaves; since her delight is flown,
For whom should she have waked the sullen year?
To Phoebus was not Hyacinth so dear
Nor to himself Narcissus, as to both
Thou, Adonais: wan they stand and sere
Amid the faint companions of their youth,
With dew all turned to tears; odour, to sighing ruth.

XVII

Thy spirit's sister, the lorn nightingale
Mourns not her mate with such melodious pain;
Not so the eagle, who like thee could scale
Heaven, and could nourish in the sun's domain
Her mighty youth with morning, doth complain,
Soaring and screaming round her empty nest,
As Albion wails for thee: the curse of Cain
Light on his head who pierced thy innocent breast,
And scared the angel soul that was its earthly guest!

XVIII

Ah, woe is me! Winter is come and gone,
But grief returns with the revolving year;
The airs and streams renew their joyous tone;
The ants, the bees, the swallows reappear;
Fresh leaves and flowers deck the dead Seasons'
    bier;
The amorous birds now pair in every brake,
And build their mossy homes in field and brere;
And the green lizard, and the golden snake,
Like unimprisoned flames, out of their trance awake.

XIX

Through wood and stream and field and hill and
    Ocean
A quickening life from the Earth's heart has burst
As it has ever done, with change and motion,
From the great morning of the world when first
God dawned on Chaos; in its stream immersed,
The lamps of Heaven flash with a softer light;
All baser things pant with life's sacred thirst;
Diffuse themselves; and spend in love's delight,
The beauty and the joy of their renewèd might.

XX

The leprous corpse, touched by this spirit tender,
Exhales itself in flowers of gentle breath;
Like incarnations of the stars, when splendour
Is changed to fragrance, they illumine death
And mock the merry worm that wakes beneath;
Nought we know, dies. Shall that alone which
    knows
Be as a sword consumed before the sheath
By sightless lightning? – the intense atom glows
A moment, then is quenched in a most cold repose.

XXI

Alas! that all we loved of him should be,
But for our grief, as if it had not been,
And grief itself be mortal! Woe is me!
Whence are we, and why are we? of what scene
The actors or spectators? Great and mean
Meet massed in death, who lends what life must
    borrow.
As long as skies are blue, and fields are green,
Evening must usher night, night urge the morrow,
Month follow month with woe, and year wake year to
    sorrow.

* * *

ALFRED TENNYSON
From *In Memoriam*

II

Old Yew, which graspest at the stones
 That name the under-lying dead,
 Thy fibres net the dreamless head,
Thy roots are wrapt about the bones.

The seasons bring the flower again,
 And bring the firstling to the flock;
 And in the dusk of thee, the clock
Beats out the little lives of men.

O not for thee the glow, the bloom,
 Who changest not in any gale,
 Nor branding summer suns avail
To touch thy thousand years of gloom:

And gazing on thee, sullen tree,
 Sick for thy stubborn hardihood,
 I seem to fail from out my blood
And grow incorporate into thee.

VII

Dark house, by which once more I stand
   Here in the long unlovely street,
   Doors, where my heart was used to beat
So quickly, waiting for a hand,

A hand that can be clasp'd no more –
   Behold me, for I cannot sleep,
   And like a guilty thing I creep
At earliest morning to the door.

He is not here; but far away
   The noise of life begins again,
   And ghastly thro' the drizzling rain
On the bald street breaks the blank day.

XI

Calm is the morn without a sound,
  Calm as to suit a calmer grief,
  And only thro' the faded leaf
The chestnut pattering to the ground:

Calm and deep peace on this high wold,
  And on these dews that drench the furze,
  And all the silvery gossamers
That twinkle into green and gold:

Calm and still light on yon great plain
  That sweeps with all its autumn bowers,
  And crowded farms and lessening towers,
To mingle with the bounding main:

Calm and deep peace in this wide air,
  These leaves that redden to the fall;
  And in my heart, if calm at all,
If any calm, a calm despair:

Calm on the seas, and silver sleep,
  And waves that sway themselves in rest,
  And dead calm in that noble breast
Which heaves but with the heaving deep.

'Tis well; 'tis something; we may stand
   Where he in English earth is laid,
   And from his ashes may be made
The violet of his native land.

'Tis little; but it looks in truth
   As if the quiet bones were blest
   Among familiar names to rest
And in the places of his youth.

Come then, pure hands, and bear the head
   That sleeps or wears the mask of sleep,
   And come, whatever loves to weep,
And hear the ritual of the dead.

Ah, yet ev'n yet, if this might be,
   I, falling on his faithful heart,
   Would breathing thro' his lips impart
The life that almost dies in me;

That dies not, but endures with pain,
   And slowly forms the firmer mind,
   Treasuring the look it cannot find,
The words that are not heard again.

XXVII

I envy not in any moods
   The captive void of noble rage,
   The linnet born within the cage,
That never knew the summer woods:

I envy not the beast that takes
   His license in the field of time,
   Unfetter'd by the sense of crime,
To whom a conscience never wakes;

Nor, what may count itself as blest,
   The heart that never plighted troth
   But stagnates in the weeds of sloth;
Nor any want-begotten rest.

I hold it true, whate'er befall;
   I feel it, when I sorrow most;
   'Tis better to have loved and lost
Than never to have loved at all.

L

Be near me when my light is low,
   When the blood creeps, and the nerves prick
   And tingle; and the heart is sick,
And all the wheels of Being slow.

Be near me when the sensuous frame
   Is rack'd with pangs that conquer trust;
   And Time, a maniac scattering dust,
And Life, a Fury slinging flame.

Be near me when my faith is dry,
   And men the flies of latter spring,
   That lay their eggs, and sting and sing
And weave their petty cells and die.

Be near me when I fade away,
   To point the term of human strife,
   And on the low dark verge of life
The twilight of eternal day.

LIV

Oh yet we trust that somehow good
  Will be the final goal of ill,
  To pangs of nature, sins of will,
Defects of doubt, and taints of blood;

That nothing walks with aimless feet;
  That not one life shall be destroy'd,
  Or cast as rubbish to the void,
When God hath made the pile complete;

That not a worm is cloven in vain;
  That not a moth with vain desire
  Is shrivell'd in a fruitless fire,
Or but subserves another's gain.

Behold, we know not anything;
  I can but trust that good shall fall
  At last – far off – at last, to all,
And every winter change to spring.

So runs my dream: but what am I?
  An infant crying in the night:
  An infant crying for the light:
And with no language but a cry.

LV

The wish, that of the living whole
  No life may fail beyond the grave,
  Derives it not from what we have
The likest God within the soul?

Are God and Nature then at strife,
  That Nature lends such evil dreams?
  So careful of the type she seems,
So careless of the single life;

That I, considering everywhere
  Her secret meaning in her deeds,
  And finding that of fifty seeds
She often brings but one to bear,

I falter where I firmly trod,
  And falling with my weight of cares
  Upon the great world's altar-stairs
That slope thro' darkness up to God,

I stretch lame hands of faith, and grope,
  And gather dust and chaff, and call
  To what I feel is Lord of all,
And faintly trust the larger hope.

LVI

'So careful of the type?' but no.
    From scarpèd cliff and quarried stone
    She cries, 'A thousand types are gone:
I care for nothing, all shall go.

'Thou makest thine appeal to me:
    I bring to life, I bring to death:
    The spirit does but mean the breath:
I know no more.' And he, shall he,

Man, her last work, who seem'd so fair,
    Such splendid purpose in his eyes,
    Who roll'd the psalm to wintry skies,
Who built him fanes of fruitless prayer,

Who trusted God was love indeed
    And love Creation's final law –
    Tho' Nature, red in tooth and claw
With ravine, shriek'd against his creed –

Who loved, who suffer'd countless ills,
    Who battled for the True, the Just,
    Be blown about the desert dust,
Or seal'd within the iron hills?

No more? A monster then, a dream,
    A discord. Dragons of the prime,
    That tare each other in their slime,
Were mellow music match'd with him.

O life as futile, then, as frail!
  O for thy voice to soothe and bless!
  What hope of answer, or redress?
Behind the veil, behind the veil.

XCV

By night we linger'd on the lawn,
  For underfoot the herb was dry;
  And genial warmth; and o'er the sky
The silvery haze of summer drawn;

And calm that let the tapers burn
  Unwavering: not a cricket chirr'd:
  The brook alone far-off was heard,
And on the board the fluttering urn:

And bats went round in fragrant skies,
  And wheel'd or lit the filmy shapes
  That haunt the dusk, with ermine capes
And woolly breasts and beaded eyes;

While now we sang old songs that peal'd
  From knoll to knoll, where, couch'd at ease,
  The white kine glimmer'd, and the trees
Laid their dark arms about the field.

But when those others, one by one,
  Withdrew themselves from me and night,
  And in the house light after light
Went out, and I was all alone,

A hunger seized my heart; I read
    Of that glad year which once had been,
    In those fall'n leaves which kept their green,
The noble letters of the dead:

And strangely on the silence broke
    The silent-speaking words, and strange
    Was love's dumb cry defying change
To test his worth; and strangely spoke

The faith, the vigour, bold to dwell
    On doubts that drive the coward back,
    And keen through wordy snares to track
Suggestion to her inmost cell.

So word by word, and line by line,
    The dead man touch'd me from the past,
    And all at once it seem'd at last
His living soul was flash'd on mine,

And mine in his was wound, and whirl'd
    About empyreal heights of thought,
    And came on that which is, and caught
The deep pulsations of the world,

Æonian music measuring out
    The steps of Time – the shocks of chance –
    The blows of Death. At length my trance
Was cancell'd, stricken through with doubt.

Vague words! but ah, how hard to frame
   In matter-moulded forms of speech,
   Or ev'n for intellect to reach
Through memory that which I became:

Till now the doubtful dusk reveal'd
   The knolls once more where, couch'd at ease,
   The white kine glimmer'd, and the trees
Laid their dark arms about the field:

And suck'd from out the distant gloom
   A breeze began to tremble o'er
   The large leaves of the sycamore,
And fluctuate all the still perfume;

And gathering freshlier overhead,
   Rock'd the full-foliaged elms, and swung
   The heavy-folded rose, and flung
The lilies to and fro and said,

'The dawn, the dawn,' and died away;
   And East and West, without a breath,
   Mix'd their dim lights, like life and death,
To broaden into boundless day.

MATTHEW ARNOLD
Thyrsis

A monody, to commemorate the author's friend, Arthur Hugh
Clough, who died at Florence, 1861

How changed is here each spot man makes or fills!
  In the two Hinkseys nothing keeps the same;
    The village street its haunted mansion lacks,
  And from the sign is gone Sibylla's name,
    And from the roofs the twisted chimney-stacks –
      Are ye too changed, ye hills?
  See, 'tis no foot of unfamiliar men
    To-night from Oxford up your pathway strays!
    Here came I often, often, in old days –
  Thyrsis and I; we still had Thyrsis then.

Runs it not here, the track by Childsworth Farm,
  Past the high wood, to where the elm-tree crowns
    The hill behind whose ridge the sunset flames?
  The signal-elm, that looks on Ilsley Downs,
    The Vale, the three lone weirs, the youthful
      Thames? –
    This winter-eve is warm,
  Humid the air! leafless, yet soft as spring,
    The tender purple spray on copse and briers!
    And that sweet city with her dreaming spires,
  She needs not June for beauty's heightening,

Lovely all times she lies, lovely to-night! –
  Only, methinks, some loss of habit's power
    Befalls me wandering through this upland dim.
Once pass'd I blindfold here, at any hour;
    Now seldom come I, since I came with him.
      That single elm-tree bright
Against the west – I miss it! is it gone?
    We prized it dearly; while it stood, we said,
    Our friend, the Gipsy-Scholar, was not dead;
While the tree lived, he in these fields lived on.

Too rare, too rare, grow now my visits here,
  But once I knew each field, each flower, each stick;
    And with the country-folk acquaintance made
By barn in threshing-time, by new-built rick.
    Here, too, our shepherd-pipes we first assay'd.
      Ah me! this many a year
My pipe is lost, my shepherd's holiday!
    Needs must I lose them, needs with heavy heart
    Into the world and wave of men depart;
But Thyrsis of his own will went away.

It irk'd him to be here, he could not rest.
   He loved each simple joy the country yields,
     He loved his mates; but yet he could not keep,
For that a shadow lour'd on the fields,
     Here with the shepherds and the silly sheep.
       Some life of men unblest
He knew, which made him droop, and fill'd his head.
     He went; his piping took a troubled sound
     Of storms that rage outside our happy ground;
He could not wait their passing, he is dead.

So, some tempestuous morn in early June,
   When the year's primal burst of bloom is o'er,
     Before the roses and the longest day –
When garden-walks and all the grassy floor
     With blossoms red and white of fallen May
       And chestnut-flowers are strewn –
So have I heard the cuckoo's parting cry,
     From the wet field, through the vext garden-trees,
     Come with the volleying rain and tossing breeze:
The bloom is gone, and with the bloom go I!

Too quick despairer, wherefore wilt thou go?
　　Soon will the high Midsummer pomps come on,
　　　Soon will the musk carnations break and swell,
　　Soon shall we have gold-dusted snapdragon,
　　　Sweet-William with his homely cottage-smell,
　　　　And stocks in fragrant blow;
　　Roses that down the alleys shine afar,
　　　And open, jasmine-muffled lattices,
　　　And groups under the dreaming garden-trees,
　　And the full moon, and the white evening-star.

He hearkens not! light comer, he is flown!
　　What matters it? next year he will return,
　　　And we shall have him in the sweet spring-days,
　　With whitening hedges, and uncrumpling fern,
　　　And blue-bells trembling by the forest-ways,
　　　　And scent of hay new-mown.
　　But Thyrsis never more we swains shall see;
　　　See him come back, and cut a smoother reed,
　　　And blow a strain the world at last shall heed –
　　For Time, not Corydon, hath conquer'd thee!

Alack, for Corydon no rival now! –
  But when Sicilian shepherds lost a mate,
    Some good survivor with his flute would go,
  Piping a ditty sad for Bion's fate;
    And cross the unpermitted ferry's flow,
      And relax Pluto's brow,
  And make leap up with joy the beauteous head
    Of Proserpine, among whose crowned hair
    Are flowers first open'd on Sicilian air,
  And flute his friend, like Orpheus, from the dead.

O easy access to the hearer's grace
  When Dorian shepherds sang to Proserpine!
    For she herself had trod Sicilian fields,
  She knew the Dorian water's gush divine,
    She knew each lily white which Enna yields,
      Each rose with blushing face;
  She loved the Dorian pipe, the Dorian strain.
    But ah, of our poor Thames she never heard!
    Her foot the Cumner cowslips never stirr'd;
  And we should tease her with our plaint in vain!

Well! wind-dispersed and vain the words will be,
    Yet, Thyrsis, let me give my grief its hour
        In the old haunt, and find our tree-topp'd hill!
Who, if not I, for questing here hath power?
    I know the wood which hides the daffodil,
        I know the Fyfield tree,
I know what white, what purple fritillaries
    The grassy harvest of the river-fields,
        Above by Ensham, down by Sandford, yields,
And what sedged brooks are Thames's tributaries;

I know these slopes; who knows them if not I? –
    But many a dingle on the loved hill-side,
        With thorns once studded, old, white-blossom'd
            trees,
    Where thick the cowslips grew, and far descried
        High tower'd the spikes of purple orchises,
            Hath since our day put by
    The coronals of that forgotten time;
        Down each green bank hath gone the
            ploughboy's team,
    And only in the hidden brookside gleam
Primroses, orphans of the flowery prime.

Where is the girl, who by the boatman's door,
　　Above the locks, above the boating throng,
　　　　Unmoor'd our skiff when through the Wytham
　　　　　flats,
　　Red loosestrife and blond meadow-sweet among
　　　　And darting swallows and light water-gnats,
　　　　　We track'd the shy Thames shore?
　　Where are the mowers, who, as the tiny swell
　　　　Of our boat passing heaved the river-grass,
　　　　Stood with suspended scythe to see us pass? –
　　They all are gone, and thou art gone as well!

Yes, thou art gone! and round me too the night
　　In ever-nearing circle weaves her shade.
　　　　I see her veil draw soft across the day,
　　I feel her slowly chilling breath invade
　　　　The cheek grown thin, the brown hair sprent
　　　　　with grey;
　　　　　I feel her finger light
　　Laid pausefully upon life's headlong train; –
　　　　The foot less prompt to meet the morning dew,
　　　　The heart less bounding at emotion new,
　　And hope, once crush'd, less quick to spring again.

And long the way appears, which seem'd so short
   To the less practised eye of sanguine youth;
      And high the mountain-tops, in cloudy air,
   The mountain-tops where is the throne of Truth,
      Tops in life's morning-sun so bright and bare!
         Unbreachable the fort
   Of the long-batter'd world uplifts its wall;
      And strange and vain the earthly turmoil grows,
      And near and real the charm of thy repose,
   And night as welcome as a friend would fall.

But hush! the upland hath a sudden loss
   Of quiet! – Look, adown the dusk hill-side,
      A troop of Oxford hunters going home,
   As in old days, jovial and talking, ride!
      From hunting with the Berkshire hounds they
         come.
         Quick! let me fly, and cross
   Into yon farther field! – 'Tis done; and see,
      Back'd by the sunset, which doth glorify
      The orange and pale violet evening-sky,
   Bare on its lonely ridge, the Tree! the Tree!

I take the omen! Eve lets down her veil,
    The white fog creeps from bush to bush about,
        The west unflushes, the high stars grow bright,
    And in the scatter'd farms the lights come out.
        I cannot reach the signal-tree to-night,
            Yet, happy omen, hail!
    Hear it from thy broad lucent Arno-vale
        (For there thine earth-forgetting eyelids keep
        The morningless and unawakening sleep
    Under the flowery oleanders pale),

Hear it, O Thyrsis, still our tree is there! –
    Ah, vain! These English fields, this upland dim,
        These brambles pale with mist engarlanded,
        That lone, sky-pointing tree, are not for him;
    To a boon southern country he is fled,
            And now in happier air,
    Wandering with the great Mother's train divine
        (And purer or more subtle soul than thee,
        I trow, the mighty Mother doth not see)
    Within a folding of the Apennine,

Thou hearest the immortal chants of old! –
    Putting his sickle to the perilous grain
        In the hot cornfield of the Phrygian king,
    For thee the Lityerses-song again
        Young Daphnis with his silver voice doth sing;
            Sings his Sicilian fold,
    His sheep, his hapless love, his blinded eyes –
        And how a call celestial round him rang,
        And heavenward from the fountain-brink he
            sprang,
    And all the marvel of the golden skies.

There thou art gone, and me thou leavest here
    Sole in these fields! yet will I not despair.
        Despair I will not, while I yet descry
    'Neath the mild canopy of English air
        That lonely tree against the western sky.
            Still, still, these slopes, 'tis clear,
    Our Gipsy-Scholar haunts, outliving thee!
        Fields where soft sheep from cages pull the hay,
        Woods with anemonies in flower till May,
    Know him a wanderer still; then why not me?

A fugitive and gracious light he seeks,
    Shy to illumine; and I seek it too.
        This does not come with houses or with gold,
    With place, with honour, and a flattering crew;
        'Tis not in the world's market bought and sold –
            But the smooth-slipping weeks
    Drop by, and leave its seeker still untired;
        Out of the heed of mortals he is gone,
        He wends unfollow'd, he must house alone;
    Yet on he fares, by his own heart inspired.

Thou too, O Thyrsis, on like quest wast bound;
    Thou wanderedst with me for a little hour!
        Men gave thee nothing; but this happy quest,
    If men esteem'd thee feeble, gave thee power,
        If men procured thee trouble, gave thee rest.
            And this rude Cumner ground,
    Its fir-topped Hurst, its farms, its quiet fields,
        Here camst thou in thy jocund youthful time,
        Here was thine height of strength, thy golden
            prime!
    And still the haunt beloved a virtue yields.

What though the music of thy rustic flute
   Kept not for long its happy, country tone;
      Lost it too soon, and learnt a stormy note
Of men contention-tost, of men who groan,
      Which task'd thy pipe too sore, and tired thy
         throat –
         It fail'd, and thou wast mute!
Yet hadst thou alway visions of our light,
      And long with men of care thou couldst not stay,
      And soon thy foot resumed its wandering way,
Left human haunt, and on alone till night.

Too rare, too rare, grow now my visits here!
   'Mid city-noise, not, as with thee of yore,
      Thyrsis! in reach of sheep-bells is my home.
   – Then through the great town's harsh,   heart-
wearying roar,
      Let in thy voice a whisper often come,
         To chase fatigue and fear:
   Why faintest thou? I wander'd till I died.
      Roam on! The light we sought is shining still.
      Dost thou ask proof? Our tree yet crowns the hill,
   Our Scholar travels yet the loved hill-side.

THOMAS HARDY
The Going

Why did you give no hint that night
That quickly after the morrow's dawn,
And calmly, as if indifferent quite,
You would close your term here, up and be gone
   Where I could not follow
   With wing of swallow
To gain one glimpse of you ever anon!

   Never to bid good-bye,
   Or lip me the softest call,
Or utter a wish for a word, while I
Saw morning harden upon the wall,
   Unmoved, unknowing
   That your great going
Had place that moment, and altered all.

Why do you make me leave the house
And think for a breath it is you I see
At the end of the alley of bending boughs
Where so often at dusk you used to be;
   Till in darkening dankness
   The yawning blankness
Of the perspective sickens me!

You were she who abode
   By those red-veined rocks far West,
You were the swan-necked one who rode
Along the beetling Beeny Crest,
   And, reining nigh me,
   Would muse and eye me,
While Life unrolled us its very best.

Why, then, latterly did we not speak,
Did we not think of those days long dead,
And ere your vanishing strive to seek
That time's renewal? We might have said,
   'In this bright spring weather
   We'll visit together
Those places that once we visited.'

   Well, well! All's past amend,
   Unchangeable. It must go.
I seem but a dead man held on end
To sink down soon . . . O you could not know
   That such swift fleeing
   No soul foreseeing –
Not even I – would undo me so!

THOMAS HARDY
Places

Nobody says: Ah, that is the place
Where chanced, in the hollow of years ago,
What none of the Three Towns cared to know –
The birth of a little girl of grace –
The sweetest the house saw, first or last;
   Yet it was so
   On that day long past.

Nobody thinks: There, there she lay
In a room by the Hoe, like the bud of a flower,
And listened, just after the bedtime hour,
To the stammering chimes that used to play
The quaint Old Hundred-and-Thirteenth tune
   In Saint Andrew's tower
   Night, morn, and noon.

Nobody calls to mind that here
Upon Boterel Hill, where the waggoners skid,
With cheeks whose airy flush outbid
Fresh fruit in bloom, and free of fear,
She cantered down, as if she must fall
   (Though she never did),
   To the charm of all.

Nay: one there is to whom these things,
That nobody else's mind calls back,
Have a savour that scenes in being lack,
And a presence more than the actual brings;
To whom to-day is beneaped and stale,
  And its urgent clack
  But a vapid tale.

THOMAS HARDY
After a Journey

Hereto I come to view a voiceless ghost;
   Whither, O whither will its whim now draw me?
Up the cliff, down, till I'm lonely, lost,
   And the unseen waters' ejaculations awe me.
Where you will next be there's no knowing,
   Facing round about me everywhere,
     With your nut-coloured hair,
And gray eyes, and rose-flush coming and going.

Yes: I have re-entered your olden haunts at last;
   Through the years, through the dead scenes I have
     tracked you;
What have you now found to say of our past –
   Scanned across the dark space wherein I have lacked
     you?
Summer gave us sweets, but autumn wrought division?
   Things were not lastly as firstly well
     With us twain, you tell?
But all's closed now, despite Time's derision.

I see what you are doing: you are leading me on
    To the spots we knew when we haunted here
        together,
The waterfall, above which the mist-bow shone
    And the then fair hour in the then fair weather,
And the cave just under, with a voice still so hollow
    That it seems to call out to me from forty years ago,
        When you were all aglow,
And not the thin ghost that I now frailly follow!

Ignorant of what there is flitting here to see,
    The waked birds preen and the seals flop lazily;
Soon you will have, Dear, to vanish from me,
    For the stars close their shutters and the dawn
        whitens hazily.
Trust me, I mind not, though Life lours,
    The bringing me here; nay, bring me here again!
        I am just the same as when
Our days were a joy, and our paths through flowers.

THOMAS HARDY
The Walk

You did not walk with me
Of late to the hill-top tree
  By the gated ways,
  As in earlier days;
  You were weak and lame,
  So you never came,
And I went alone, and I did not mind,
Not thinking of you as left behind.

I walked up there to-day
Just in the former way;
  Surveyed around
  The familiar ground
  By myself again;
  What difference, then?
Only that underlying sense
Of the look of a room on returning thence.

THOMAS HARDY
The Voice

Woman much missed, how you call to me, call to me,
Saying that now you are not as you were
When you had changed from the one who was all to
   me,
But as at first, when our day was fair.

Can it be you that I hear? Let me view you, then,
Standing as when I drew near to the town
Where you would wait for me: yes, as I knew you
   then,
Even to the original air-blue gown!

Or is it only the breeze, in its listlessness
Travelling across the wet mead to me here,
You being ever dissolved to wan wistlessness,
Heard no more again far or near?

   Thus I; faltering forward,
   Leaves around me falling,
Wind oozing thin through the thorn from norward,
   And the woman calling.